Character Based Management

A Key to More Productive & Effective Organizations

Robert Beezat

First published by Dog Ear Publishing
4011 Vincennes Rd
Indianapolis, IN 46268
www.dogearpublishing.net

ISBN: 978-1-4575-4664-8

This book is printed on acid-free paper.

Printed in the United States of America

TABLE OF CONTENTS

CHARACTER BASED MANAGEMENT

A Key to More Productive & Effective Organizations

CHAPTER ONE

THE HUMAN SIDE OF MANAGEMENT

Think of the worst boss you ever had. Picture that person. Write down three things that boss did which made her or him a poor supervisor/manager.

If you can, do that right now before you read any further.

When I picture the worst boss I ever had, the first thing that comes to mind is that I wanted to leap across the desk and punch him.

I knew that was a bad career move, so I never did it.

But when I think about why I wanted to punch him, here are the first three things that come to mind:

- **Everything was about him**...his ideas...his goals...his image...his success.

- **He did not want others to look good**...he was threatened that anyone who worked for him, or with him, would look better than him, and would get in the way of his moving up in the organization. Therefore, he would not do much to help you or others, and he would often do things to undermine your success or the success of others.

- **He was a phony**...he constantly spouted management sayings that sounded good e.g., "Let's approach this on a win-win basis," which we all knew really meant that he wanted to win and didn't care at all if you or anyone else won anything.

And that is just the beginning of the list. I could add many more. In addition to my own list, I have facilitated quite a few supervisory and management training courses over the years. During those training sessions, I always ask the trainees to list three characteristics of the worst boss they ever had. Here are some of the other terms that people usually list:

Liar…selfish…lazy…doesn't care…autocratic…has favorites…screams and yells a lot…doesn't listen…bullies…intimidates…doesn't communicate…explodes…demeaning…won't try anything new…dismisses your ideas…unpredictable…induces fear…and many more adjectives and phrases which are unprintable.

Fortunately, I have also had some good bosses over the years. When I think of them, many positive things come to mind. Here are the first three:

- **They wanted me to succeed** and they helped me do so.

- **They took the time to listen and help me solve problems** I was dealing with.

- **They treated me and my co-workers with respect**, which brought out the best in us.

And just like the bad list, the students I taught and I can add many more positive characteristics of the good bosses we have had over the years:

Honest…fills you in on things…keeps you in the loop…stands up for you…gets you the resources you need to do the job…treats everyone the same…is a good motivator…disciplines in private…understands your family needs…treats you with respect…wants to hear new ideas on how to improve things…cares about her or his people…good communicator.

What both of these lists show is that most of what makes someone a good boss is not their technical skills or job-related knowledge, though both are important.

What makes them a good or bad boss are their interpersonal behaviors, which either help or hinder the success of the organization they serve, the people they lead, and the people with whom they work.

These positive and negative behaviors greatly influence the performance of individual employees, groups of employees, and, in fact, the success of the entire organization.

So, at this point it is important to ask where do these bad and good behaviors come from? Are they just behaviors we pick up along the way by following the examples of our supervisors? Or do they reflect who and what we are as a person and, in turn, how we think about ourselves and others? Do our behaviors reflect our character? And if so, what do we mean by a person's character?

About This Book

The premise of this book is that our behaviors reflect our character. And our character greatly influences the quality and effectiveness of our decisions and the success of the people and organizations we manage.

In this book, I will explore with you the following topics:

- The idea of moral character. What does the term mean and how does good moral character impact the workplace?
- What is management and what does it have to do with moral character and the success of an organization?
- How do we build good moral character?
- The importance of integrating personal behavior, management process skills, and technical knowledge.

- Communication, leadership, and decision-making behaviors and techniques which reflect and promote good character in yourself and build a high functioning team with and among the people you manage.

During my career, I have seen innumerable management theories and systems which were supposed to solve problems and overcome the obstacles organizations face in being profitable, effective, and efficient.

The first system which I learned about was PPBS (Program Planning Budgeting System) which was introduced at Ford Motor Company in the late 1950's by then CEO Robert McNamara. PPBS was the first of many alphabet soup acronyms which were supposed to transform an organization. MBO (Management By Objectives) came along in the late 1960's. That was followed by TQM (Total Quality Management), Six Sigma, The Four E's of Leadership, SWOT, SMART, PDCA, MBWA, Re-Engineering, Right-Sizing, and many, many more systems which most of the time helped organizations to some degree. Most of the theories were purported to be relatively quick fixes to the many complex challenges facing organizations. They usually proposed three or four simple things you needed to do to turn around your organization.

Almost all of the theories had some good points which had positive impacts on organizational effectiveness and success. But these various theories usually did not deliver on their grandiose promises regarding how this or that theory would make the organization more effective and successful. Often, they only addressed one portion of the total organizational culture, processes and operation. As systems, they were frequently dumped after several years because they did not solve as many of the organizational management challenges as they were purported to solve. That is why a new alphabet soup theory came along a few years later to replace the previous one.

Another reason that many of these systems failed is they only recommended changes in the surface behavior of managers. They did not look into the intellectual and inter-personal sources of such behavior. This approach is typified by the "One Minute Manager" books. These books generally recommended good practices for supervisors to use in managing people, but they did not require the manager to embody those behaviors in her or his character.

Most people can spot a phony, particularly when they see a person say one thing and then do another thing over a period of time. The problem with the "One Minute Manager" books was that managers were told to adopt certain behaviors as quick-fix practices. However, those one minute behaviors did nothing to change the basic character of the manager. For example, as I mentioned earlier, I had a boss who was always talking about looking at situations from a "win-win" approach. That sounded good, and when he first started using that terminology we thought it was a positive concept and had the potential to make us a more cohesive and productive team. However, after a few weeks of "win-win" comments, we realized that it was just more "BS." Winning meant that he'd won. He did not care if the rest of us ever won. Surface changes which do not reflect the real character of the manager as exhibited in their many other negative behaviors are recognized by employees. They just add to the lack of credibility and effectiveness of the manager.

That is why I am writing this book. In all of the books I have read, management workshops and seminars I have attended, and top management and leadership people I have spoken with, I have never heard anyone propose a theory of management that made the moral character of managers in an organization an integral part of helping to drive organizational success.

This book will provide a framework for thinking about and doing things which improve the moral character of managers, and in turn help organizations become more effective and successful by unleashing

CHAPTER TWO

CHARACTER AND MANAGEMENT: FOCUS ON MANAGEMENT

"If it weren't for the people, this job would be easy."

A very experienced manager told me that during my first year as a manager. I chuckled when he said it, but over the years of managing organizations in business, government and the not-for-profit sectors, I learned he was absolutely right.

It is the people in an organization who present the biggest challenge to managers.

The people also present the biggest opportunities for a manager to achieve a successful and high-performing organization, which brings a great deal of job satisfaction to the manager and the people they manage.

Defining Management

Management is basically getting work done with and through others that one person cannot do alone.

An organization's greatest asset is its people.

In most organizations it is also the largest cost factor.

Maximizing the contributions of the people who work in the organization should be one of the top priorities of managers.

Maximizing employee contributions should not just be about the volume of work that each individual performs.

It should also be about tapping into and unleashing the individual and collective intelligence, initiative, and creativity of those employees.

Bringing out the best in employees takes a manager who is truly interested in the well-being of staff. The manager must recognize, respect, and appreciate the talents that each employee brings to the job.

Management is Both an Art and a Science

What is commonly referred to as the science of management are the activities related to Process Skills and Job Knowledge.

The art of management focuses more on Inter-Personal Behaviors.

Most of us get quite a bit of training in the science of management. We go to school to learn many aspects of it. We attend in-house and external, work-related training classes. There are many books and videos which help us increase our management process skills and job knowledge.

All of that learning and training is important.

The art of management builds upon a solid foundation in the science of management.

In any type of art, the artist needs to know the fundamentals or science of their craft. That is why we all need excellent Job Knowledge, and we must be aware of the best techniques available to improve our Process Skills.

One of my favorite quotes about artists is attributed to Pablo Picasso. Someone once asked Picasso what he and other great artists talked about when they got together. The questioner thought Picasso would respond by talking about theories of art, and how creativity takes place and results in great art.

Picasso's response to the question is that the artists discussed what was the best paint thinner and where you could get it.

That question and answer illustrated that artists cannot produce great art of any kind unless they know the fundamental materials and techniques of their craft.

Once an artist knows the fundamentals of their craft and keeps them current, the artist can then create something beautiful. The artist can translate their vision of what is possible into something that other people also experience as beautiful.

Creating something beautiful is the goal of art. One of the basic characteristics of something beautiful is that it brings into harmony a diversity of elements. In painting, the artist brings together many different elements: color, texture, shadow, light, perspective, etc. In music a composer brings into harmony a wide variety of sounds from many different instruments, sometimes including the human voice(s) as well as words/lyrics.

Though it is not usually considered art, I have always found it interesting that scientists, when they finally develop and prove a complex scientific theory, call the theory beautiful. They do so because they have brought together many diverse facts and theories into a new and complete whole.

Along those lines, I often think of a quote from Albert Einstein when asked to define genius. One of his answers is: "The ability to see the connection between things that no one else has seen." Einstein saw the connection between energy, mass, and the speed of light ($E=MC2$). By seeing those connections he changed much of the world we live in.

Most of us will never be great painters, sculptors, singers, musicians, actors, etc. But many of us can be great artists in how we manage employees.

Getting people to work together to their maximum ability, using all of their diverse knowledge, talents, and skills, is also a thing of beauty. It takes conscious effort on the part of a manager to create that successful, productive, effective, and yes, beautiful team.

Managing For Individual and Team Success

Most people start a job with a lot of enthusiasm. They like the mission and vision of the organization. The new workers think they have the education, background and experience to contribute to achieving the organization's goals and objectives. They look to succeed in their job, helping the organization succeed, and eventually helping themselves grow and develop their talents and skills within the organization in order to get raises, promotions, and job satisfaction.

Unfortunately, and way too often, organizations beat those high aspirations out of people, but not as a matter of policy. No organization would consciously adopt such a stance toward their employees. But, it becomes a reality because managers in many organizations do not recognize that good management is based first on the real and perceived character of all management personnel.

When I started working on a full-time basis after completing college, I was amazed at how much time was wasted by me and my co-workers moaning and complaining about how poorly we were being treated by our bosses. Many complaints were about unfair and unprofessional treatment, but some complaints and frustrations were about how we were ignored or thwarted when we suggested that some changes be made to the way the company or organization did things. We thought we could make our work easier and more productive, and create a positive and maybe even fun, work environment.

3. **How similar the management issues were across all sectors of employment.**
   - Unless someone specifically referred to the current organization they worked for, it was not possible to tell whether they came from the private, governmental, educational or not-for-profit sectors.
   - All of the organizations faced one or more of the same issues and challenges to be as effective as they wanted to be.

4. **The great variety of management systems and tools that were used by different organizations.**
   - There was no perfect system or management tool which helped every organization.
   - Different systems worked best in different organizations depending on a variety of factors.

5. **The success of new management systems and tools were closely related to how the employees were involved in developing and implementing them.**

   - Top-down imposition of a new system was often fought by the people most affected by it.
   - Inclusion of input from all workers at all levels of the organization increased employee "buy-in" to the new system.
   - "Buy-in" bred commitment to change and the best efforts of the employees to make the new system work.
   - The organization became more successful when everyone in the organization was committed to making positive change.

Managing people is both an art and a science. We can get better at it.

We do not succeed all of the time, but we greatly increase our opportunity for success if we are always learning and developing those positive character traits that define a good manager.

CHAPTER THREE

CHARACTER AND MANAGEMENT: FOCUS ON CHARACTER

Moral Character

The concept of "character" is a difficult term to define.

Webster's dictionary defines character as "the complex of mental and ethical traits marking and often individualizing a person."

Character can be good or bad, and most of the time it is a mix of both good and bad characteristics. No one is perfect, and none of us will become perfect in the future.

We call someone a person of good character when they generally behave in ways which we find admirable and promote good outcomes.

We call someone a person of bad character when they generally behave in ways that most of us find dislikable and result in negative outcomes.

My definition adds a few more elements to the Webster definition: Character is...

- The result of a mixture of our knowledge, philosophies, beliefs, life experiences and interpersonal relationships which we have encountered in our lives.
- This complex mixture forms our values and habits.
- Our values and habits are then expressed in our behaviors and actions.

Here is a list of some behaviors and actions that most of us would include in describing a person of good character:

- Honesty
- Integrity
- Genuineness
- Truthfulness
- Trustworthiness
- Dependability
- Kindness
- Respect for and appreciation of others' humanity
- Not self-involved

There are many more positive behaviors we attribute to a person of good character. This is just a first list that comes to my mind when thinking about a person of good character. If we go back to the first chapter of this book, we can see a more extensive list of characteristics of good managers.

Another way to think about good moral character is to look back in the history of ideas and philosophies which speak about the qualities of good character. One of the first written explorations of these qualities was by the early Greeks. They wrote about the four cardinal virtues upon which all of our actions are built and that we should take into account. They are:

- **Wisdom/Prudence** – the ability to use our heads and our hearts to understand and make judgments and decisions between possible courses of action at a given time in a particular situation.

- **Justice** - fairness, equity, and giving and receiving what is properly due individuals and groups.

- **Temperance** - restraint, balance, the practice of self-control, abstention, and moderation tempering the appetites.

- **Courage** - fortitude, forbearance, strength, endurance and the ability to confront fear, uncertainty and intimidation.

Almost every philosophical and religious tradition honors and promotes these habits of mind, heart, and action which we attribute to a person of high moral character.

Starting to Think About Character and the Workplace

There are two things I am most proud of as a manager over the years.

First, that my top management team in one organization I managed started to call themselves "The Dream Team." The reference is to the 1992 USA Olympic basketball team that won the Gold Medal. The team won every game they played in the Olympics by an unprecedented and unsurpassed average victory margin of 44 points.

Though we have all gone in different directions since we worked together, the members of that management group still refer to themselves as "The Dream Team." They fondly and proudly recall how many challenges we successfully faced and overcame as a total organization and within each of their own areas of responsibility with the teams they managed.

Second, is what an accounting clerk said to me and all of those in attendance at a going-away party before I departed for another position. She said, "Bob, you bring out the best in people." I was stunned when she said that. I had never looked at managing people from that perspective. I was also humbled by the statement, and said to myself, "You'd better live up to that in the future."

I have thought about that compliment many times since. I wondered if there was a connection between who we are at our deepest core and how we manage people. About 10 years later, I was teaching a course titled "Principles of Management" at a university in the Chicago area. As part of that class, we looked at the history of organizational management. One of the first writers about management theory and practice was Henri Fayol (1841-1925). While teaching the class, I read the following quote from Henri Fayol in a textbook we used for the class. It made me think more seriously and deeply about the possible connection between moral character and managing an effective and successful organization.

> "In making decisions... the moral character (of the decision-maker)... determines the quality of the decisions."

Wow! That is something I never heard before when reading, talking, and thinking about management theories and practices.

I wondered: "Who is Henri Fayol, and what does he mean by that statement?"

Henri Fayol, Moral Character and the Workplace

After a little research, I learned that Henri Fayol was a French mining engineer and director of mines who developed a general theory of business administration that is often called Fayolism. He and his colleagues developed this theory in Europe in the late 1800s and early 1900s. That was about the same time as Frederick Taylor developed his similar but more well-known theory of scientific management in America. Taylor's work is widely acknowledged as the foundation of modern management methods. But as I looked into it a little more, I saw that Fayol's work was just as important as the work of Taylor.

As stated by L. Urwick in the Foreword to the 1949 publication of Fayol's *General and Industrial Management*, "The work of Fayol and Taylor was, of course, complementary. They both realized that the problem of personnel and its management *at all levels* (text is italicized in the original) is the "key" to industrial success. Both applied scientific method to this problem. That Taylor worked primarily on the operative level from the bottom of the industrial hierarchy upwards, while Fayol concentrated on the Managing Director and worked downwards, was merely a reflection of their very different career paths.".

Fayol's work was one of the first comprehensive statements of a general theory of management which he published in 1916. He wrote that there were six primary functions of management and fourteen principles of management as follows:

6 Functions of management

1. Plan
2. Organize
3. Staff
4. Command or Direct
5. Coordinate
6. Control

14 Principles of management

1. Division of labor
2. Authority
3. Discipline
4. Unity of command
5. Unity of direction
6. Subordination
7. Remuneration
8. Centralization

9. Chain of command
10. Order
11. Equity
12. Stability of tenure of personnel
13. Initiative
14. Esprit de corps

Many of these terms and ideas are still part of the common language used today when thinking about how to manage an organization, but neither the list of functions nor principles of management said anything directly about moral character and the quality of decisions. So, I looked more deeply into his quote.

As I read Fayol's book, I found that though he never directly defined moral character, he had comments sprinkled throughout his text which he thought were the characteristics and behaviors that illustrate good moral character as a key factor in the success of an organization. Here is a sampling of those characteristics and behaviors he mentions:

Equity	Loyalty	Tact
Firmness	Impartiality	Energy and Good
Initiative	Care for Common	Health
Dignity	Good	Persistent, Thoughtful
Moral Courage	Drive	Determination
Foresight	Justice	Always Learning
Kindliness	Willingness to Accept	
Flexible	Responsibility	

This list of characteristics and behaviors closely mirrors the list modern-day employees consider when distinguishing their "best boss" from their "worst boss," which was set forth in the first chapter of this book.

Among all of those characteristics of a good manager, Fayol is particularly concerned with Equity, which he says "results from the combination of kindliness and justice. Equity excludes neither forcefulness nor sternness, and application of it requires much good sense, experience and good nature... Desire for equity and equality of treatment are aspirations to be taken into account in dealing with employees... the head of the business must frequently summon up his highest faculties... to instill a sense of equity throughout all levels of the scalar chain (i.e., the chain of command)."

According to Fayol, being a manager of good moral character does not mean being a pushover and acquiescing to the needs of the employees no matter what those needs are. The manager sometimes has to be forceful or stern as situations may call for.

To be a good manager, "the head of the business must frequently summon up her or his highest faculties." Those words reminded me of a quote I read many years ago that President John F. Kennedy adapted from the Greek philosophers: "The ancient Greek definition of Happiness is the full use of all of your powers along the lines of Excellence."

A good manager of an organization and its people can experience great job satisfaction and happiness if they use the full range of their powers at a very high level/excellence. I think that is the particular joy of being a good manager. We use everything we have: our mind, our skills, our body, our experience, our learning and everything else about ourselves, to make an organization successful. If we experience that joy and satisfaction as a manager, our employees will find it works for them as well. But it is up to us as managers to model that behavior and encourage it in our employees.

Fayol asks managers to constantly develop all of these skills by observing these qualities in more experienced managers and con-

We learn from the people around us and our relationships with them.

In today's world, we learn more and more from electronic stimuli.

Learning is good. But everything we learn is not the truth.

An important part of being a person of good character is to understand as much of true reality as we can, and then act accordingly.

If we act based on true information, we can make choices and decisions that will make our own situation, and/or the situation of the people we manage, more positive and successful.

If we act based on untrue information, our choices and decisions will make things worse.

So, it is extremely important that we are always seeking to know as much of the truth as we can about every bit of reality we encounter.

And, it is very important to realize that, frequently, we do not know the whole truth.

To illustrate that point, I like to look at knowledge along a continuum. Here is an example of my continuum of knowledge on several topics:

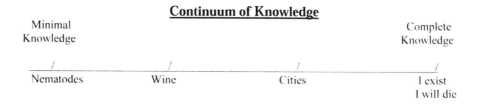

I am 100% certain that I exist and that I will die. I know hardly anything about nematodes as well as many other topics. I know quite a bit about cities, because part of my career was as a municipal management consultant. In that capacity, I have worked with close to 350 cities around the US. I know a little about wine. I prefer red to white wine. I know it is pleasurable and relaxing to have a glass of wine with dinner. Beyond that, I could never tell you what is a good, mediocre or bad wine, and why they are designated to be so.

Most of what I know about most things is less than complete knowledge. That is important to keep in mind when making choices and decisions. And that is why, particularly in an organizational setting as a manager, the more honest views of reality we can elicit from the people we manage, the better chance we, the people we manage, and the entire organization have of making quality decisions to help the organization be successful.

Beliefs

Since we, as individuals and as groups, do not usually understand the total truth/reality with which we are dealing, we often fill that gap with beliefs.

Some people say they believe in nothing, by which they usually mean they don't believe in God or anything that is spiritual. And that is fine. But that is just one area of belief.

Most of us believe that we will be alive tomorrow. We don't know that for sure. There is plenty of evidence that life is risky. We could be in a car accident. We could have a heart attack. Someone may walk into our workplace and starting shooting people.

However, based on our knowledge, our past experience and the credibility of who tells us things, we believe that certain things are true and will occur. But we are not 100% certain.

As is the case with knowledge, I think it is also helpful to think of belief along a continuum as follows.

Continuum of Belief

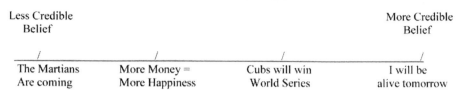

Less Credible Belief ·· More Credible Belief

| The Martians Are coming | More Money = More Happiness | Cubs will win World Series | I will be alive tomorrow |

The odds are I will be alive tomorrow. But I could die in a car accident this evening. Being a Chicago native, I believe the Cubs will win a World Series once in my lifetime. Money is important, but once we have enough to meet our basic needs, other aspects of our lives bring more happiness than just accumulating more money. And though there may be some extraterrestrial life in the universe, it is not likely that it will be coming to visit us from Mars.

As is the case with knowledge, we also make choices and decisions based on our beliefs. If I believed I would not be alive tomorrow, I would stop writing this book and spend time with my loved ones. If I was certain that the Cubs would play in and win the World Series next year, I would buy season tickets so I would be assured of seeing them win the World Series in person. If I believed that more money would equal more happiness, I would have made many different decisions throughout my life regarding the work I chose to do and the compensation I would have earned. Nothing more needs to be said about the belief statement that "The Martians are coming!"

What we know and what we believe are two foundations upon which our character is built.

The closer our knowledge and beliefs get us to understanding reality as it really is and not as we hope or wish it is, the better chance we have of making quality decisions that will produce positive outcomes for ourselves and the people we manage.

Emotions

Emotions are psychological and physical reactions to our perceptions of reality.

Many choices and decisions we make are driven as much by how we feel as by what we think.

Emotions are more than just feelings. Most of the time, they accurately encapsulate our knowledge of reality without going through a long, logical analysis.

This almost instantaneous "gut feeling" spurs us to immediate action.

If we see a large wild animal running toward us, our mind and body react simultaneously, and we start running to a safe place. If our emotions did not spur us to this quick reaction, we would probably end up as the large animal's lunch.

On the other hand, if we see an old friend walking toward us, our body relaxes, a smile lights up our face, and we often quicken our step to greet our friend with a handshake or a hug.

The mind-body connection as expressed through emotions should not be dismissed as unimportant or inconsequential when it comes to how our character develops and how we act, particularly in stressful situations.

Emotions are significant drivers of our behavior. They usually become our automatic response to similar situations. In many matters, our emotions help us quickly deal with both negative and positive perceptions of realities that confront us.

But they can also become habits that eliminate rational analysis of different situations as we face them.

We have to recognize those emotional habits in ourselves, and whether or not they serve us and the people we manage in a positive way.

We have to be careful to not act on our emotional responses when a situation does not call for it.

Again, think about your worst boss. What are your feelings when you think about her or him?

They are often a mix of many negative feelings such as dread, anger, hate, powerlessness, fear, etc. Those emotional reactions limit our ability to work as positively as possible with that boss.

On the other hand, when we think of our best boss, we are filled with positive emotions of friendliness, respect, cooperativeness, accomplishment, fun, etc. These emotional reactions lead us to work positively with that boss.

How we feel about ourselves, others, and different aspects of reality plays a very significant role in how we engage with all of reality.

Just as what we know and believe are not always a completely accurate understanding of reality, our emotions and feelings are not always appropriate responses to the people and situations which confront us.

We need to understand what our emotional reactions are to different people and different work situations.

We need to think about why we have those particular emotional responses.

We have to determine whether or not those emotional reactions are helping or hurting us in making good decisions that successfully manage people and organizations.

Then, where necessary and appropriate, we need to train ourselves to change our emotional reactions so that our emotions are not a hindrance, but contribute to good character and good management.

Relationships

We are social beings.

We do not exist in isolation.

We do not thrive in isolation.

We exist and thrive as part of broad social and economic networks and relationships that make life possible.

It is no different in the workplace.

Management is getting work done through and by others that one person cannot do alone.

In order to be successful, managers must understand the high importance of building and sustaining positive relationships with and among the people they manage.

As illustrated in the comments from employees in Chapter One in this book, so many of the negative traits associated with being a bad boss are related to the bosses' unawareness of and/or inability to build positive and mutually supportive relationships with and among the people they manage.

That unawareness and/or inability is the source of most management problems in an organization.

Conversely, so many of the traits described by people in Chapter One that are associated with a good boss are related to building and maintaining positive and mutually supportive interpersonal relationships.

People know when someone truly cares for and respects them. They know, too, when their boss pays only lip service to these qualities and behaviors.

An important element in understanding our character is to recognize our human ability and capacity to create and nourish mutually supportive and caring human relationships.

Then we must do things that increase our own capacity to create and sustain positive human relationships.

We must do things which create an environment where the people we manage are encouraged to grow and use their own capacity to develop mutually supportive and productive relationships with the people with whom they work and, where applicable, people who work for them.

Role Models

One way we learn is by watching others.

If we want to get good at something, we look for role models.

When I was a kid and wanted to be a better baseball player, I watched guys who were older than me and were successful ball players.

I copied their batting stance, how they pitched, and how they fielded the ball.

I also watched how they carried themselves.

Were they confident without being cocky? How did they respond to pressure? Did their teammates look at them as leaders? And if they did, what did this person do to earn that respect?

It was the same in the classroom.

I wanted to be a good student. I watched my older sister, who was a good student, to see how she studied. I observed and thought about how other good students handled themselves in the classroom. I looked to see what teachers thought was important in a good student.

I also thought about what made a teacher a great teacher. Why did I really look forward to the class taught by a great teacher compared to the ho-hum class taught by an ordinary teacher? It was usually a combination of what they knew (command of the subject matter), but more importantly, it was because they loved the subject they were teaching, and they wanted you to love and enjoy it also.

It is no different when it comes to work.

We want to learn from good role models, particularly when we are young and starting out in the work world. We want to see who succeeds and how they do it.

Most of us have had good and bad bosses.

We enjoy working for good bosses.

We start looking for another job when we have a bad boss, and it looks like they will be around for a while.

I have been fortunate to have worked for several good bosses. When I worked for them, I did not take it for granted. I wanted to learn from them and follow their example.

I observed how they did things in terms of managing me and my co-workers. I tried to copy their behaviors when I dealt with co-workers.

Sometimes I asked them why they did some of the things that made them a good boss. They were usually glad to take a few minutes to discuss with me their ideas and approaches to managing people successfully.

Conversely, when I had bad bosses, I observed and thought about how they conducted themselves. I learned what not to do. But unlike with the good bosses, I never asked them why they dealt with people in such negative ways. I needed to keep my job, at least until I got a new boss or I found another job.

Our character has many sources as described above.

But what our character is today will change.

It can change for better or worse.

That is up to each of us.

We can improve our character by:
- Increasing our knowledge
- Examining and refining our beliefs

- Understanding and modifying our emotions
- Building positive relationships with people, and
- Looking for, paying attention to, and learning from good role models.

CHAPTER FIVE

IMPROVING CHARACTER: GROW OUR MIND EVERYDAY

No Three-Step, Quick-Fix Shortcuts

Simple, easy solutions have minimal positive impact on us as individuals or on the people and organizations we manage.

This book does not propose simple and easy solutions.

It has taken us a lifetime to develop our character to what it is today.

It will take significant time and effort to improve our character, and to have it pay off in increased organizational effectiveness and personal job satisfaction.

But there are some things we can start doing immediately that will begin to improve our character and start to become noticeable to the people we manage.

The first thing we can do is to:

"Shut Up and Listen"

That is the message I have on a yellow Post-It note inside the work portfolio I carry around with me.

It is a constant reminder that the key to learning is being a good listener.

I learned early in my career that I had a tendency to talk too much in meetings.

I wanted to communicate to others what I thought the situation was and how we could fix it.

But as I watched other good managers and leaders I worked with or for, I started to understand that an important part of their success in solving problems and getting people to work together was that they did two things:

- First, they listened to everyone who had some ideas regarding what the problem was.

- Second, they elicited ideas from everyone regarding how the problem could be resolved.

Once that information was freely and openly discussed by all of the participants in a meeting, a positive solution was generally reached by consensus. It was almost always a better solution than the one I was thinking about before the meeting.

It was better because it took more factors into account, some of which I'd never thought about until someone else in the discussion raised the point.

It was also better because the collective input resulted in determining a course of action which had a better chance of succeeding. It had the best efforts of everyone who was part of arriving at the decision to make it work.

Increase Our Knowledge and Understanding Every Day

An open and inquiring mind is one element of being a person of good character.

In this day of "Big Data," we are constantly inundated with new information.

aspects. As mentioned earlier, Einstein's definition of genius is to see the connections between things that no one else sees.

Increasing our knowledge and understanding does not mean simply academic training.

We should be seeking to grow our mind every day in many different ways:

- <u>Read and View as Broadly as Possible</u>. Don't limit yourself to the same sources of information day after day. Too many websites, TV, videos and magazines are targeted to reinforce our perceptions of reality. It takes more conscious effort to expose ourselves to new and different areas of knowledge.

- <u>Seek to Put the Joy and Wonder Back into Our Learning</u>. When is the last time you were simply awed by learning something new? When did you start to learn about a new topic and could not stop.

- <u>Listen To and Exchange Ideas With a Broad Range of People</u>. We tend to hang out with the same people every day. That is pretty normal. Who has the time to be always interacting with new people? At the same, there are frequently opportunities to engage with different people having different ideas and experiences than we have. There are professional associations, neighborhood and community groups, service clubs, volunteer opportunities, lectures, and many other in-person ways to meet, talk with, and learn from each other. There are also many media-based opportunities with which to meet and learn from others.

- <u>Meditate as Part of Your Daily Routine</u>. No matter how much new information we are exposed to and learn, we need to synthesize that knowledge. We need to think about the knowledge we have acquired and see how it fits with what we knew before. It is hard to do that in the hustle and bustle of everyday activities. There is a growing body of neurological and brain research that shows the connections between what we learn, how we behave and how meditation helps us deepen our learning. Meditation also helps us improve our listening skills. It helps us see the inter-connectedness of many aspects of reality.

- <u>Write Out What You Have Learned</u>. Writing helps us clarify and synthesize what we are learning. Putting ideas on paper makes ideas real.

What all this knowledge and understanding leads to is wisdom.

Wisdom is the ability to use our heads, our hearts, and our cumulative experience to understand, make judgments, and make decisions between possible courses of action in a particular situation.

Wisdom ties together what we know, what we love and care for, and our practical life experience to make the best possible judgment of what to do.

Wisdom is not gained by sitting in an ivory tower thinking great thoughts.

Wisdom results in practical action.

CHAPTER SIX

IMPROVING CHARACTER: GROW OUR HEART EVERYDAY

Though it may seem inappropriate to say this in the context of the workplace, building positive relationships is based on our ability to love and be loved.

Love in the workplace?

Really? Love?

What does love have to do with the workplace?

Just as our knowledge, beliefs, and emotions drive our choices and decisions, so does our capacity for and practice of love.

Love Broadly Defined

First, it is important to recognize that in our culture, love is too often too narrowly defined and identified with physical and erotic love.

But there are many other forms of love, most of which we are familiar with:
- A parent's love for a child
- A family's love for each other
- A friend's love for a friend
- A self-less love for others
- A team's love for each other

According to almost all religious, spiritual, and philosophical institutions and systems, love should be understood in broader terms which affect many different aspects of our lives.

Buddhists use the terms interdependence, compassion, and empathy. Philosophers, psychologists, and even some economists use the term altruism. Businesses often use the term teamwork. And championship sports teams of all kinds attribute their success to teamwork and team chemistry.

The ancient Greeks proposed that there are six types of love:
- **Romantic** – Erotic/Physical
- **Friendship** – Individual, Groups, Teams
- **Playful** – Social/Fun, Playing Games, Bar Banter
- **Long Term** – Deep Mutual Understanding and Support
- **Selfless** – Charity for the benefit of others
- **Self** – Caring for self and spreading love outward

Except for the romantic aspects of love, the other five aspects are very applicable to building and maintaining positive relationships in the workplace.

We all want to love and be loved. It is a huge part of who and what we are as human beings.

I define love very broadly as follows:

- Relational connection between people that is
- Mutually open to and accepting of other people,
- Desires and acts for the well-being of other people, and
- Unites people in supportive communities.

Let's look at this definition in terms of management and the workplace. And while doing so, keep in mind the following characteristics of a bad boss and good boss as described by many employees in Chapter One:

Bad Boss

Liar...selfish...lazy...doesn't care...autocratic...has favorites...screams and yells a lot...doesn't listen...bullies...intimidates... doesn't communicate...explodes...demeaning...won't try anything new...dismisses your ideas...unpredictable...induces fear

Good Boss

Honest...fills you in on things...keeps you in the loop...stands up for you...gets you the resources you need to do the job...treats everyone the same...is a good motivator...disciplines in private...understands your family needs...treats you with respect...wants to hear new ideas on how to improve things...cares about her or his people...good communicator.

Relational Connection Between People

Management is getting work done by and with others which cannot be accomplished alone.

A workplace consists of many human relationships. Here are some examples:

- Vertical/hierarchical such as a manager and subordinates
- Horizontal/peer to peer
- Limited within a particular work group or division of an organization
- Broad inter-divisional that may function across the entire organization
- External with customers and clients

Clearly, human relationships are one of the most important elements that must be recognized and dealt with in any organization.

Everyone in an organization has a responsibility to make relationships work. But it is particularly the job of managers at every level of the organization to create a work environment where human relationships are positive and contribute to achieving the goals of the organization. If we do that, we bring out the best in people as individuals and as groups, and more will be accomplished than anyone thought possible.

Mutually Open To And Accepting Of Other People

We do not have to like someone to work productively with that person. Being open to and accepting of others does not mean that we have to like everything about her or him.

But we have to see them as unique human beings who are of value and worthy of respect in and of themselves.

If we are going to have positive human relationships, both parties (individuals and/or groups) have to accept people as they are, not as we think they are or we wish they were.

Think of yourself when you meet someone for the first time.

When you do that, you want to be accepted by the other person for who you are: a human person who is worthy of the other person's respect.

You are you, and you want to be accepted on that basis.

That does not mean you think you are perfect. None of us is. But you see yourself as a whole person with a personality, life experiences, and knowledge worthy of respect and acceptance.

If we want that for ourselves, then so do others with whom we work.

Unlike our personal relationships, at work we do not choose who we will be in relationship with. Other people are simply there, and we have to find ways to make our relationships successful and productive.

We can't fake this type of openness and acceptance.

We know when we are accepted and respected as someone of value, and so do the people we manage.

Therefore, it is extremely important to have a perspective about people that sees them as deserving of acceptance and respect. Managers have to model that attitude and behavior. Once subordinates see that it works, they will begin to mirror that attitude and behavior with their manager, co-workers, and where applicable with their subordinates.

Desires & Acts For The Well-Being Of Other People

Love is about making choices.

It is much more than a feeling.

Sometimes love is accompanied by positive feelings of warmth, closeness, and mutual support. But most times, whether in our personal lives or at work, those types of feelings are not present. We are too focused on getting something done. How we feel about someone at a particular time is not relevant to the task at hand.

Whether or not our feelings are positive or negative, we can make choices to do things that promote

- Just our own well-being,
- The well-being of the other person, or
- Our mutual well-being.

All three of these options are available to us. Ideally, choosing our mutual well-being is the optimal choice, particularly in work situations.

To choose to do something that is mutually beneficial, we have to communicate with each other. That means not only sharing our thoughts with someone else, but also hearing and understanding what they want done. We have to hear not just what they say, but what they mean.

Unites People In Supportive Communities

Generally, guys don't talk about love with other guys.

It is not the manly thing to do.

But I always find it interesting how often members of a winning sports team talk about how they are a family, and in many instances how they love one another. I just saw a comment in the sports section of the newspaper where the star pitcher on a team talked about how the team really loves one another, and that was a key factor in why the team was doing so well.

Nobody objects or is surprised when a star athlete says that.

If it is okay in our culture to love your teammates when you're playing a sport, why not use the word love when we are talking about our teammates at work?

As I mentioned earlier in this book, there have been hundreds of management systems and tools introduced to organizations of all types over the last 50 years. One of the few that has had remarkable staying power is the idea of building teams within an organization.

The idea and practice of creating and sustaining teams has stuck around because it works. Successful teams:

- Take the best of what everyone on the team has to offer.
- Communicate well among each other.
- Work together as a unit to reach a common goal.
- Achieve much more than they would alone.

Who wouldn't want that as a manager or an employee?

Mixing Work, Love, And Friendship

Maybe, instead of talking about love in the workplace, it is better to talk about friendship.

When people become friends, there is a bond created between them. It is built on trust, caring, and mutual support. A bond is created which can last a lifetime. It is hard to define this bond, just as it is hard to define love.

But people know when it exists, and they know when that bond is respected and proactively maintained. We all respond positively to someone who really cares about and wants what is good for us. That is the case in our personal lives, and can and should be the case in our work lives.

Most of us have made good friends over the years with the people we work with. In fact for many of us, friendships we make at work are some of the most important and long-lasting friendships we enjoy even when we no longer work with the person or persons.

Management, Friendship, And Discipline

As the top manager in several organizations, I have had friendships with many people up and down the organizational hierarchy. I never had a problem giving directives to any of them when I had to. I never hesitated to discipline a subordinate if I had to.

I know that friendship is often frowned upon when applied to the relationship between a manager and the people they supervise. That is usually based on the theory that if we are friends with our subordinates, we will not able to correct or direct them as managers need to do from time to time.

I find that line of reasoning to be faulty. One of the aspects of a good friendship is that both parties recognize appropriate boundaries, whether at work or in their private lives. Also, if employees are consistently treated with respect and know that we want the best for them and from them, having conversations about improving performance can be done successfully. In fact, it not only does not harm the personal and professional relationship, it enhances it.

The reason I do not see a conflict between friendship and disciplining subordinates is that I look at what the word "discipline" means and where it comes from. I think too often when we hear the word discipline, we almost always think of punishment. However, the Latin root of the word discipline is "disciplina," which means to teach or instruct. The word disciple also comes from this same root word. So I always looked at discipline first and foremost as an opportunity for me to teach, and the employee to learn, how to be a better employee. Certainly punishment can be a part of discipline. But if we think of discipline primarily as a teaching and learning opportunity, engaging in conversation with an employee regarding how they can become a better employee is the way to start. Punishment can, and occasionally must, be used as a way to improve performance, but it should not be the starting point.

As a manager we have responsibilities to the organization we serve. As a manager and a fellow human being, we have responsibilities to care for the people we manage. I call that caring, love. Others may call it friendship. Others may call it positive human relationships. No matter what we call it, unfortunately, many managers think very little about creating and maintaining positive human relationships with and among the people they manage.

That is a great loss to the organization.

CHAPTER SEVEN

CHARACTER AND COMMUNICATION

Open and honest communication with the people we manage is one of the most important factors in the success of an organization.

It does the following:

- Brings out the best ideas from everyone in the organization regarding:
  - Defining a problem
  - Solving a problem
  - Getting work done more efficiently and effectively

- Builds the commitment from everyone to the goals of the organization

- Maximizes the contributions of each person in the group

- Develops employees' talents, knowledge, and skills

- Provides a high level of job satisfaction to the manager and the people they manage

What manager would not want all of the above to happen among the people they manage?

There are many books written about the techniques and processes of good communication. I will touch on a few of those topics later in this chapter.

But no communication technique or process will work if staff doesn't believe the manager is a person of good character.

They will not trust us.

And, if they do not trust us, they will not openly share their ideas and maximize their efforts to attain the goals we all want to achieve for the organization.

So, the first words we should always think of regarding communication when it comes to gaining the trust of the people we manage is to:

Shut Up and Listen!

I mentioned this message on a Post-it note to myself earlier in this book when discussing how important it is for a manager to be learning by listening.

Just as listening is so important to learning in general, it is most important in communicating with the people we manage.

As the old adage goes: "We have two ears and one mouth. Divide your communication time accordingly."

Listen Deeply to Understand

Our best chance of solving a problem when there is a disagreement about some matter is to listen closely to the person or persons with whom we have a difference.

Try to understand what they are saying.

Don't be thinking of counter arguments.

Don't be thinking how wrong they are.

Try to understand what they fear if a decision is made that they are opposing.

The first thing people say when they are opposed to something is not always their deepest reason.

People often oppose something because they are afraid of how the decision will hurt them or the organization.

In order to find out what it is that they fear, we must listen deeply and attentively to understand what they are saying.

We have to give them all the time they need to explain their concerns. Though the time spent at the beginning of this type of conversation may seem too time consuming, it is worth taking the time for two reasons:

1.   Unless sufficient time is taken to hear what the employee is concerned about, the employee will think and feel that they have not been really heard and understood.

2.   If we invest the time now, we will almost always save much more time later on in terms of gaining the respect of and input from this employee in the future; and we will not have to revisit the problem we are trying to solve.

We have to ask them questions to clarify what they mean if we do not understand what they are saying.

Finally, we have to tell them what we think they are saying and see if we understand it fully.

Once both of us agree on what the other person is concerned about, we can then usually tell them what we are concerned about.

If we have treated them civilly and with respect, they will usually give us the same treatment.

At this point, we can agree that we understand each other. We do not have to agree with how each of us sees the matter.

Once both of us respect each other and understand what each of us fears, then we can usually start working together to find a solution.

Listening Takes Time

Most of us often feel pressure at work to get things done quickly. That is one reason we tell people what to do instead of taking the time to get their input on what needs to be done and how it might be done better.

On some occasions, a decision needs to be made immediately, and it is the manager's job to make a decision quickly.

But many decisions do not have to be made immediately.

We do so anyway.

We do it out of habit or because of the bad example set by our managers.

Listening Takes Courage

We often make decisions quickly and on our own because we think we will look weak or indecisive if we fail to make an immediate decision.

Getting input and ideas from the people we manage will almost always result in a better solution and a stronger, more engaged, and more motivated work group.

And rather than appearing weak to our employees, our willingness to take input will make us look confident and strong.

It is Up to the Manager to Make Open Communication Work

The manager has to lead this process of interchange. Employees are not in a position to conduct such a discussion unless the manager initiates it and guides it along.

Once we go through this process several times without negative consequences for them, employees will trust us and gain the confidence to express themselves openly and positively, and problems can be avoided or resolved as soon as practicable.

Employees will see that we are persons open to input, not afraid of disagreement from subordinates, and who respect and genuinely want to work with them to help make them and the organization as successful as it can be.

Investing time in the people we manage will pay off in increased production, creativity, initiative and commitment.

Investing time communicating with the people we manage gives us the best chance to solve a problem or make an improvement the first time we try to do so.

Do What You Say You Are Going to Do

Nothing builds trust faster or stronger with the people we manage than doing what we say we are going to do, particularly as it relates to them.

One of the things I always did when I started a new management position was to meet individually with the people who reported directly to me to see what I could do to help them do their job. They might need some financial resources, or be having a hard time getting along and working with a peer, or have an employee who was not performing satisfactorily. Sometimes it was as simple as getting a piece of office equipment or a water fountain installed in a place which was more convenient and time saving from a work standpoint. Sometimes it was a work process which the employee had to put up with because it was the preference of their previous boss. The list of possible things that employees wanted to change or make better could be anything. Often, it was more than one thing.

If I listened well, I could always pick out something that was important to them and that, in my position as their manager, I could help them resolve. It did not have to be the largest matter on their plate. But I would pick out one thing after that conversation; and then, sometime over the next several days, weeks or even months for some of the larger matters, I would work with that employee to help them resolve the issue they were dealing with.

The people I managed started to gain confidence in our working relationship. They would then bring more issues to our discussions, and we would work together to resolve them.

One of the things I learned early on in managing people was that most of the people we manage already have a pretty good idea of how to resolve a problem.

When I had my first management job running an organization of close to 150 people and a total budget of about $10,000,000 (in 1970 dollars), I was 28 years old. Every one of the managers who reported to me were in their 40's and 50's, and had been doing their jobs for 10, 15 or 20 plus years. I wondered how I could manage people who knew so much more about their area of work and had many years of experience doing that work.

The first time a manager who reported to me came to me with a problem he was struggling with (about two weeks after I started in my new job), he knocked on my door and asked if he could come in. I said yes, so he closed the door and started telling me about a situation in which one of his subordinates was causing problems for the other employees in the work group.

I thought to myself, what the heck can I tell this guy who knows his area of work and the people he supervises better than I do?

So I listened to what he was concerned about.

I asked him some questions so I was sure I understood the issue.

I then asked him what he thought could or should be done.

He had several ideas, but he was not sure how to proceed. And he was not too sure how to proceed for two reasons:

1. He wasn't sure what would work best.

2. He was concerned that if he made the wrong decision it would make him look bad to the group he supervised, the employee who was causing the problem, and me, his manager.

We talked about the several alternatives he was considering.

I then discussed with him how what he was proposing would fit into the overall management of the organization as I knew it at the time. I also suggested some ideas which he had not thought about before. By the time that discussion was complete, he knew exactly what he was going to do. But now he had more confidence in his decision, and he had the support of his manager (me).

He went out of my office and began to handle the situation in a way that helped that employee perform better. The group he managed saw how he handled the situation and they began to work together better.

Create an Environment Where Your People Can Succeed

When people you manage have such a successful experience, they usually share that with some of their peers. Soon, all the people who report to you begin to see you as someone who is a resource and can help them solve their problems.

Very importantly, they start to take the same approach with the people they manage. They start listening to each other as well as to the employees they manage. New ideas bubble up all the time. People are not afraid to share their knowledge and experience with each other. People come to work thinking about how things can be done better. They take the initiative to solve problems and create new opportunities for success for themselves and the people they work with.

Don't Let Yourself Be Distracted

It tells an employee that you are not interested in what your employees have to say if you are distracted while conversing with them.

Turn away from your electronic video screens. Mute your phone. Don't look at other papers on your desk.

Focus your attention on the person you are conversing with… and stay focused.

Open Body Language Facilitates Good Communication

Sit or stand in a relaxed, open, and attentive posture.

Look people in the eyes when talking with them.

Links Between Character and Communication

People judge us based on how we communicate with and act toward them.

Our character plays a large role in how we communicate with and act toward other people.

And, how we perceive ourselves and others as human beings is a huge factor in how our character is determined.

One key to being a person of character and integrity is based on what we think about people in general.

So, let's think a little about who and what people are.

What are your thoughts about other people? Are people of intrinsic value based on who and what they are? Are they worthy of respect? Do they deserve to be treated with dignity? Do they have knowledge, experience, and ideas that are of value in getting work done effectively and efficiently?

Or are other people basically lazy time-wasters who want to do the minimum to keep their jobs?

There are many evolutionary, philosophical, and theological/religious views of who and what constitutes a human being. I am not going to discuss those ideas in the context of this book. However, for those who are interested in this topic and want to read and think about it in more depth, I have written another book titled: *Knowing and Loving: The Keys to Real Happiness.*

A good place to start thinking about others is, "Respect others as you wish to be respected." Think about why you want to be respected. Is it because you think you are smarter than others? Or that you have more experience in some areas than others? Those are legitimate reasons to command respect.

But if you think deeply about it, you want to be respected because you think that is what you deserve. And you think you deserve it because you are a human being. There are qualities about us as human beings that we think are worthy of respect. Not just what we do as human beings, but who and what we are. I think each of us is a unique person who deserves respect. We have the capacity to know and love.

If we truly have the viewpoint about ourselves and other people that we all deserve respect, it becomes part of our character. How we communicate and work with the people we manage will reflect our true character. The people we manage will know very quickly whether or not we really respect them.

In summary, good communication between a manager and the people she or he manages will do the following:

- Bring all of the best information, ideas, and experience of the group to the table.
- Lead to a better solution.
- Build consensus and commitment.
- Everyone takes responsibility to get the job done.
- We only have to deal with the problem once.

CHAPTER EIGHT

CHARACTER & LEADERSHIP

There are many books about leadership and leaders. Almost all of them have some helpful things to say. I have read many of those books as they come out from year to year.

I have also learned a lot about leadership by watching other leaders and thinking about the qualities and behaviors which make them successful.

I will focus my comments on the relationship of character and leadership.

What is really most important about the link between character and leadership is that

- Who a leader is
- What the leader says, and
- How the leader behaves

have to be of a consistent piece.

The ideas, beliefs, emotions, words, and actions of a leader need to be in sync. If they are not, people will not follow that leader for long.

People can spot a phony after they interact with someone for a while, particularly in a work situation where a manager and employees come in contact with each other frequently.

Bad and Good Leaders

An important factor to keep in mind when thinking about the link between character and leadership is that leaders can be of good or bad moral character.

History is full of examples of leaders of bad moral character who inflicted a great deal of death and destruction on others.

Adolph Hitler is one of those leaders who comes to mind when thinking about a leader causing a great deal of pain and suffering. Joseph Stalin in Russia, Nero in ancient Rome, and numerous others have also led people to do terrible things.

History is also full of examples of good leaders. Mahatma Gandhi comes to mind. So does Martin Luther King, Jr. and Nelson Mandela. Many great religious and spiritual personages (Mohammed, Jesus, Moses, the Buddha and Confucius) have and still play strong leadership roles though they have been dead for many years.

There are many different definitions of leaders and leadership.

The definition that I have put together over the years of reading about leadership and leaders, and observing leaders in action, has the following elements:

- A Person
- Out in Front of
- Willing Followers
- In a Situation

A Person

That a leader is an individual is self-evident.

But what is not self-evident is that almost anyone can be a leader.

There is a never-ending debate regarding whether leaders are born or made.

In my experience, it is usually a bit of both.

Some people are born with what we consider natural leadership qualities. They want to be in front of groups. They want to determine the direction in which the group will move. They have certain personality traits that help them be leaders.

Others become leaders based on their knowledge about a topic, or their friendliness with people, or the exigencies of a situation (I will address the situational aspects of leadership later in this chapter). Sometimes, these are reluctant leaders who have had the role thrust upon them and only assume the role because they have to.

Some leaders derive their leadership role from the formal organizational structure of which they are a part. Because they are put in charge of other people as a manager, they are expected to be leaders.

Many people are promoted into management positions because they are really good workers. To some degree that makes sense. But someone who is a very good worker does not automatically become a leader because they are appointed to a leadership position. They have to learn how to be a leader, and they have to earn their leadership role. Some do. Many don't.

On the other hand, there are often informal leaders in a work group. Their leadership role is given to them by the people they work with based on a range of factors, including personality, job knowledge, job competence, and their ability to earn the respect and confidence of their fellow workers.

Out In Front Of

A leader is out in front of other people.

They are out in front of people because they have a vision of what the group wants to attain.

The leader can clearly and convincingly articulate the vision and goals in ways that make sense to and motivate the people they lead.

Very importantly, the leader not only knows where people want to go, but the leader presents practical ways and means to get there.

People follow someone they believe in.

They believe that their leader understands:

- Who they are as a group
- What they want to attain as a group, and
- How to get the group to where they want to go.

A leader has to address all three elements described above in the process of becoming a leader.

To become a successful leader, we have to understand what really motivates the people we aspire to lead. To do that, we have to pay attention and think about what motivates the group as a whole, as well as individuals in the group. We have to listen deeply to what people really want for themselves and the group.

In work situations, we assume, correctly I think, that the great majority of people we manage want to be productive and successful in their work. They want to grow their skills. They want a work environment that encourages them to give their best effort, and when possible, rewards them for their contributions. Some may want to move up the organizational ladder.

Leaders will be out in front of a group of willing followers if they understand the complexities, diversity, and depth of the people they lead.

Willing Followers

A leader without willing followers will not be a leader for long, and they will fail to accomplish as much as is possible.

Some leaders do not have willing followers because they share a vision with their followers on what needs to be done, but they do not have a plan for the practical things which need to be done to get there.

They may be visionaries, but without some practical ideas of how to get to where the group wants to go, they are not successful leaders, and will not accomplish what they and the group they wish to lead hope to do.

So, if we are going to be leaders, we not only need a vision, but we need to articulate some practical steps to take to get us and the people we lead to where we want to go.

Leadership is generally not successful if the leader takes a top down only approach to getting things done by and with people.

Some leaders do not have willing followers, because they try to impose a vision and plan on the people they wish to lead. A manager, particularly in a work situation, is expected to have goals that need to be accomplished. To be successful in these types of situations, the manager has to present the vision to the people they manage. They need to openly discuss the vision and practical steps which will be taken to achieve the goals.

After this open and respectful discussion, the leader may need to adjust their own vision for two reasons.

First, the group will often bring to the surface more and better ideas than the ones the leader started with. It really does happen...often.

Second, the leader may decide to compromise a little to get broader support from the people they manage. Compromise is often thought of as a dirty word. But when it comes to managing a group of people, compromise can keep a project moving forward, and there can be time in the future to make further adjustments.

Real leaders understand that in order to lead people, their followers must be part of defining the vision and practical things that need to be done to get the job done.

It takes courage for leaders to make changes to their own vision based on the ideas and motivation of the people they lead. Many leaders, in name only, think they will lose their leadership position and role if they yield any of their decision-making authority and role to the group. Many times, sharing decision-making with our employees actually confers more power on us as managers. Also, sharing decision-making and power with the people we manage gradually empowers them to grow in their decision-making capability as individuals and as peers with others in their work group.

Eventually, if some of the people we manage also manage people as part of their job, they, as managers, will begin to use this approach with the people they manage. Over a period of a year or two, this mode of shared communication and decision-making becomes part of the total culture of the organization. It brings out the best in everyone. More gets done, and it gets done better than before.

A trickier situation is when the vision and goals are set by managers higher in the organization and managers have no choice in, or ability to, adjust that vision and goals. In those cases, the manager has to be candid with the people they manage. They have to tell them what is going on, and how the manager and employees are expected to fit into and perform to achieve the imposed vision and goals. The leader and the group can still discuss how they think is the best way to get done what is imposed on them. In such cases, leaders earn the respect and support of the people they manage.

In A Situation

Different leadership styles and characteristics work in different situations.

General George Patton was a great military leader during WWII. Franklin Roosevelt was a great President during the war. They had very different personalities and temperaments, and possessed very different skill sets. If they switched roles, neither one would have done very well and would probably not be remembered today.

Sometimes people are leaders based on their technical knowledge and expertise. We don't usually think of accountants as leaders, but some accountants become leaders not only in their professions; but they go on to build and lead large accounting businesses.

Scientists are usually not people we think of as leaders; but again, because of their sheer genius and grasp of their subject, they become leaders in their field of study as well as in businesses which grow out of their research.

Sports teams almost always have someone who stands out as a leader. They are usually good at their sport, but not necessarily the best player on the team. But they are seen by their teammates as embodying what it takes to be successful and win.

Sometimes the circumstances demand that someone step up to lead. Martin Luther King, Jr. was a minister. He was intent on serving as a minister to people in his community. As the civil rights movement began to gather momentum, someone had to fill the role of leader. He was in the midst of some aspects of the civil rights movement, but was not the leader of it until circumstances demanded that someone become the focal point for the movement. That mantle fell on the shoulders of Martin Luther King, Jr. He accepted it, and he became one of the great leaders in American history.

To be a leader, the situation and the person have to fit together.

That is why I think most of us can be leaders if the opportunity presents itself. When that happens, it is essential to being a leader to have your character and your actions reflect who you really are in the situation which confronts you.

People have to trust a leader. They have to see that there is consistency between what the leader thinks, believes, and says, and on how the leader behaves.

As a manager in an organization, you are expected to lead. To do so, you will need to integrate everything about you and your job into a complete and consistent whole. That consistent and complete whole is your character.

At this point it is good to look again at the chart presented at the beginning of this book.

CHARACTER BASED MANAGEMENT

A Good And Successful Manager Must Integrate

Inter-Personal Behaviors	Process Skills	Job Knowledge
Values	Planning	Product or Service
Habits/Virtues	Communicating	Personnel
Character	Leading	Finance
Growth	Team Building	Technology
Continuous Learning	Organizing/	Marketing & Sales
Dealing With	Re-Organizing	Legal
Uncertainty	Managing Risk	

A very important part of being a person and manager of good character is that our actions flow from how we perceive reality. Integrity means that our values and behaviors are of one piece.

What we think, believe, and value leads to how we act. They have real-world consequences.

Integrating all of these elements and factors is a challenge. But good leaders do that well and often.

There is great job satisfaction for ourselves when we lead taking into account as many of these factors as are appropriate and helpful for a situation.

There is also great job satisfaction for the people we manage. They have the chance to grow and develop. They come to work every day thinking about how they can help make things better and more productive.

CHAPTER NINE

CHARACTER AND DECISION-MAKING

Managers have to make decisions many times throughout a day.

Some are major decisions that affect the entire organization.

Others are smaller from an organizational standpoint and may only affect one employee.

Some decisions are routine and do not require a great deal of thought. We have made these decisions before, and we are reasonably confident how they will turn out.

Some decisions are very challenging because of the complexity of the matter being addressed. We may not have made a decision regarding this matter before. And therefore, we are not absolutely certain how it will turn out.

Making decisions is a real test of our character:

- Can we withstand pressures to decide a certain way or to make a decision sooner rather than later?

- Do we have all of the information we need to make a good and appropriate decision?

- Will our decision be in concert with our values?

- Will we look weak and/or lose face if we make the wrong decision?

- Do we involve others in the decision-making process or do we go it alone?

Pretty heavy stuff. And there are no easy answers to some of those questions.

I think there are several important elements to consider when we are confronted with challenging decisions. Here are three questions to ask yourself when confronted with a situation that requires a decision:

- When do I have to make the decision?

- Do I have all the information I need to make the best decision possible at the time? If not, how can I get more information?

- Do I make the decision on my own or do I involve others in the decision-making process?

When Do I Have to Make the Decision?

This seems like a simple question.

But unless we are responding to an emergency situation (i.e., an attack in the military, a police or fire emergency call, a work-related accident, etc.) most important decisions do not have to be made immediately. In emergency situations there are generally standardized protocols in which managers and employees are extensively trained so that the correct decision will be made very quickly with a successful outcome.

Most of us are not confronted with these types of situations.

But often, when a decision needs to be made, there is a lot of pressure (self-imposed or from outside our selves) to make a decision quickly.

Resist that urge. A person of good character does not succumb to phony, external pressure.

Some decisions need to be made sooner rather than later, but many do not have to be made immediately. Take a few minutes to decide when you think a decision needs to be made. That will help you decide on the second question.

Do I have all the information I need to make the best decision possible at the time? If not, how can I get more information?

Seldom do we know everything we need to know about any situation, particularly when the decision is about people. The more information we can gather within the timeframe of making the decision, the better chance we have of making a good decision.

At this point it is good to look at the Continuum of Knowledge discussed in Chapter Four.

<u>**Continuum of Knowledge**</u>

Minimal
Knowledge

Complete
Knowledge

Many times we do not have complete knowledge about a situation or problem.

There is an old adage that "there are two sides to every story. And then there is the truth."

As a decision-maker, it is our responsibility to take the time to gather as much information as we can to accurately assess the truth of a situation within the timeframe we have in which to make the decision.

That is why "Growing Our Mind Everyday" as discussed in Chapter Five is so important. We need as much and as broad a base of knowledge as possible to place ourselves closer to the "Complete Knowledge" end of the Continuum of Knowledge as we can achieve.

One of the most important elements in getting to the "Complete Knowledge" of the continuum is to take advantage of the knowledge of those we manage.

Do I make the decision on my own or do I involve others in the decision-making process?

This is often the first element that connects your character to decision-making.

One character-related consideration regarding whether or not we include others in the decision-making process is are we afraid of looking weak or lacking sufficient knowledge, and/or losing control of the people we manage if we do not make the decision ourselves?

Another character-related consideration is whether or not we think the people we manage who will be affected by the decision should have a role in making the decision, and eventually, carrying out the decision. Do we think the people we manage are worthy of respect and are of value simply as human beings so that they should be involved in making the decision?

Do we think and act in a way that recognizes other people have experience and knowledge that can contribute to the decision-making process?

"Trust in the Wisdom of Deliberative Bodies"

When I was starting out my management career, an experienced manager told me to "trust in the wisdom of deliberative bodies."

The two key words are "Wisdom" and "Deliberative."

As discussed earlier, wisdom is the ability to use our heads, our hearts, and our cumulative experience to understand, make judgments, and make decisions between possible courses of action in a particular situation.

Wisdom is not gained by sitting in an ivory tower thinking great thoughts.

Wisdom ties together what we know, what we love and care for, and our practical life experience to make the best possible judgment of what to do.

Wisdom results in practical action.

Deliberative means being thoughtful, considering all sides and viewpoints regarding a matter.

Deliberative also means that more than one person is involved in examining a situation which will lead to making a decision. Often a deliberative body consists of many people. Each one has to have the opportunity to share their ideas for the deliberative body to come up with the best solution.

It is up to us as managers to create deliberative bodies among the people we manage. We have to model that behavior. And very importantly, we have to believe that the people we manage can contribute their wisdom to making better decisions than we would make on our own.

Again, I go back to the quote from Einstein about genius: "The ability to see the connections between things that no one else sees." The combination of us as managers and the people we manage will have a better chance to see connections between different elements which will affect a decision than any of us will do alone.

But we have to be of strong character to accept and implement such a group process.

"Do it right the first time."

Finally, deliberative also includes the idea of taking sufficient time to get it right the first time.

My dad was a carpenter, and he said that often. It was not original with him, but it sure was, and is, true. He said that you needed to have the right tools, the right materials, and a good plan, or you would have a mess on your hands.

To begin with, taking time to understand what each of us in a work group is concerned about clarifies and defines what the real problem is.

A lot of time is wasted and bad decisions are made because we do not take the time to accurately diagnose a problem.

Time is also wasted if the solution to the problem we have diagnosed is not accompanied by the best solution possible. A bad decision not only wastes time and does not fix the problem. It often makes the problem worse.

CHAPTER TEN

CHARACTER & UNCERTAINTY

How we deal with uncertainty is a key component of our character.

One of the hardest things about making tough decisions is that we are seldom certain how they will turn out.

That uncertainty can cause us to behave in arbitrary and close-minded ways, building a fortress around ourselves and our ideas.

Or we can use the uncertainty to broaden our perspective.

I have written a number of chapters which point to what I think are good ways to build our character and help us be more successful managers. I think there are many good principles and general guidelines contained in those chapters.

But like everyone else, I also experience uncertainty when it comes time to make a decision about an important and concrete matter that will affect the success of the people and organization I manage.

I think I have minimized some of the uncertainty for myself by utilizing the ideas and principles set forth previously, but I am not certain how those general principles apply to any and every particular situation which I will encounter as a manager.

I think it is worth some time to exam the idea of uncertainty.

What is uncertainty?

<u>A feeling</u> - It is an emotional response that may or may not be valid.

<u>Of fear and anxiety</u> - Both emotions are unpleasant. We want to eliminate them.

<u>That we experience when we are not sure what to do</u> - See the reasons listed below.

<u>Based on our perception that our well-being is threatened</u> - In a real life/non-theoretical situation.

<u>If we don't act in a way that protects our well-being.</u> - We must decide/choose a course of action.

Why do we experience uncertainty and how do we cope with it?

We experience uncertainty for three main reasons:
- Reality is extremely complex.
- The future is unpredictable.
- Anxiety is part of the human makeup.

<u>Reality is extremely complex.</u> Though we try to simplify things as much as we can, we can seldom comprehend the broad range of realities that confront us, particularly where human beings and human interactions are concerned. It is hard enough to understand the physical makeup of material things such as an atom, a plant, a building, a car, or anything that we interact with daily. When emotional and psychological factors enter into the picture, as well as elements of history and time, knowing everything we need to know before making a decision is near impossible. It is safe to say that in almost every important situation in our lives, we never know enough to be certain of the outcome. Hence, we feel uncertain.

<u>The future is unpredictable.</u> There are so many variables affecting most of reality that we are unable to predict how decisions on our part will be affected by them. First of all, there is just pure bad luck. Cars cross medians and hit other cars head-on and kill all of the

occupants. Also, human beings are very unpredictable. Our knowledge about ourselves is ever evolving and never complete. Our knowledge of other human beings is even less complete. So again, we experience uncertainty.

<u>Anxiety is part of the human makeup.</u> We are all familiar with the "fight or flight" reaction that we as human beings experience when confronted with threats to our well-being. It is a natural, self-preservation instinct and behavior that we all possess. Whether we chose to fight or run when we are confronted with a threat, we are uncertain of the outcome and we experience the emotions of fear and anxiety.

How Do We Cope With Uncertainty?

How we cope with uncertainty is very important to our success in managing the people and organizations for which we are responsible. I think there are three main strategies that most people adopt to deal with uncertainty:

- We distract ourselves so as not to experience the unpleasant emotions connected to uncertainty.
- We try to learn as much as possible.
- We develop a basic mindset that helps us make decisions.

<u>We distract ourselves so as not to experience the unpleasant emotions connected to uncertainty.</u> An all too frequent and easy approach to dealing with uncertainty is to distract ourselves from dealing with the underlying anxiety and fear. These distractions are easy to come by. There is a never-ending stream of stimuli to which we are all subject whether we want to be exposed to it or not.

Some people use a variety of substances to distract themselves from the underlying anxiety and fear that they experience. Drugs (illegal and prescription), alcohol, highly-caffeinated drinks and sugar-laced foods are among the many stimulants which can mask our feelings.

There is almost no end to the kinds of distractions which we are subject to or which we can actively pursue.

On the other hand, it takes our conscious choice and decision to not constantly be subject to such stimuli and distractions. Most of us are not taught that we should avoid the constant stimulation. We just take it as part of the reality in which we live. The relentless stimulation and distraction is not good for our physical, emotional, and mental health and well-being. It temporarily buries the anxiety and fear associated with uncertainty, but it takes a toll on whom and what we are and can be as flourishing human beings and good managers.

We try to learn as much as possible. Most of us seem to do reasonably well learning the practical things we need to know for our jobs and our everyday living. Depending on the nature of our jobs, we may always need to learn new things in order to perform satisfactorily and continue to make a living. The more we learn in these areas, the less uncertainty we experience in handling those aspects of our work lives. Unfortunately, many of us do not learn as much as we can about the less practical, but also very important, aspects of reality, particularly how to create, develop, and maintain positive human relationships in the workplace. For most of us, most of the time, we learn how to act and make decisions based on examples of what others do or tell us to do in order to be successful managers. Learning from example is good if we are learning from good examples that show us how to manage successfully. But too many of us have had more bad bosses than good ones. And when the pressure is on, we too often revert to the negative behaviors our bad bosses exhibited.

We develop a basic mindset which helps us make decisions. Since it is not only difficult but impossible to know everything we need to know in order to make good decisions as managers, we adopt mindsets that help us make decisions on a timely basis.

For most people this mindset is composed of several elements. It begins with some basic values that we learn from our families as we are growing up. Our formal education contributes to the development of our overall mindset, as do our jobs and social interactions with people from our work and community. Our own experience is a big contributor to our mindset. And, very importantly, there are the examples that we see of choices made by others. Choices sometimes lead to successful and happy conclusions, and other times to disaster.

Most of us adopt a mix of ideas and beliefs that guide our actions with a reasonable amount of certainty as to the outcome. The mix of ideas and beliefs allows us flexibility in addressing life's important issues based on the specifics of the situations we encounter. The mix of ideas allows us to see reality more clearly and completely, and then to respond accordingly.

Beware of "isms"

Some people, on the other hand, adopt a very specific and comprehensive set of business, management and economic ideas and/or beliefs and live by them pretty exclusively. I call them "isms." Such comprehensive mindsets in the world of management usually have an answer for every question and a prescribed course of action to take in every circumstance. The "ism" that such people adopt may speak to some issues well, and may provide a solid grounding for making some decisions and choices with great certainty.

There really are some good things about most "isms." But no "ism" is comprehensive enough to speak to all aspects of our work reality, no matter how much the proponents of the "ism" claim it to be so. That is why new management "isms" come out every few years.

In instances where the "ism" is the basis for making all decisions, the feeling of certainty is achieved, but responding to the true reality of each specific circumstance is lost. It is a trade-off many people make. They often make the trade off without realizing they are doing so. In their minds, feeling anxious and fearful is very uncomfortable for them. The certainty related to an "ism' removes that anxiety and fear.

Interestingly, there is a related internal element of uncertainty associated with every "ism," and that is the uncertainty the person who adheres to an "ism" is not doing so completely and correctly. If they do not adhere to the dictates of the "ism," they often feel guilty, fearful and/or anxious that they will be not be viewed favorably by their bosses if they do not toe the line completely and correctly. The only way to assure certainty is to adopt the "ism" wholly and completely, and make it apply to every decision and choice they make.

Being open to discerning the reality of things and situations can be scary. It does produce some anxiety and fear. But it has the great plus of allowing us to live in closer relationship to true reality in all of its complexity and variety. It also takes more time sometimes to understand a situation. It requires us to consciously form a mindset by devoting time to reading and thinking about who and what we are, and what we are encountering outside of ourselves. But the ultimate trade-off for this time and effort is an overall better set of decisions and choices that allow us and the people we manage to flourish as we/they can and should.

Summary

I like to look at certainty on a continuum, just as I did with knowledge and belief earlier in this book. I try to be at the higher end of the certainty continuum (maybe 75% or better on the scale), but I know that I won't always be there. I think all of us are seldom there if we are truly open to reality and are not trying to fit it into our preconceived "isms," ideas, beliefs, and opinions.

Continuum of Certainty

0%   100%

Certainty_____Certainty

Our certainty when it comes to making a decision can be anywhere along the line, depending on our knowledge and credible beliefs. A goal of 100% certainty, though desirable, is not always possible for reasons discussed earlier in this chapter.

We will never remove uncertainty and its related feelings of fear and anxiety from our lives entirely. But we can do several things that will help us deal with uncertainty more successfully, and which will allow us to make better decisions and choices relative to our own well-being, that of the people we manage, and the organization we serve:

1. Accept the fact that uncertainty is part of the human condition. We will never be absolutely certain of most things.

2. Do not run from, or try to hide from, the negative and uncomfortable feelings that uncertainty engenders. They are a natural part of life. They push us towards greater understanding so that we can protect ourselves from harm, and lead us to grow and flourish as human beings and managers.

3. Be open to reality. Try to understand reality as it truly is, not as we prejudge it to be or want it to be.

4. Be a lifelong learner regarding all aspects of reality, including its practical and human relationship aspects.

5. Be careful of "isms" of any kind. Some have more value and have lasted longer than others because they are more

reflective of reality, but no "ism" has the answer to every one of life's problems and challenges.

6. Don't give up the pursuit of understanding reality in exchange for getting rid of the negative feelings of fear and anxiety associated with uncertainty.

7. Evaluate situations and make decisions based on what promotes the well-being of ourselves, others, and the broader world in which we live.

8. Be quiet sometimes. Be still. Learn to be comfortable with our thoughts and with silence.

CHAPTER ELEVEN

PERSONAL & ORGANIZATIONAL IMPROVEMENT PLANS

Let's Get Practical

If, after reading the previous chapters, you think there is an important link between your character and the effectiveness of how you manage, let's think about some practical ways to improve your character so that you can:

- Bring out the best in the people you manage
- Make better decisions
- Build employee commitment to each other and the organization
- Increase productivity and effectiveness
- Increase your job satisfaction.

First of all, nothing will bring about a positive change in our character unless we consciously and deliberately take practical steps to do so.

Second, we can't do everything at one time. We need to focus on one or two areas of improvement at a time.

Here is a list of 10 behaviors we should think about on a regular basis. After reading the list, rate yourself on a scale of 1 to 5 for each Category of Improvement.

You may already be very good at some of these things, but if you are anything like me, you can still get better in some or all of them.

Plus, new people, new situations, and changes in the overall work environment constantly require us to grow as a person and as a manager of people.

Rating	Category of Improvement
_____	**1. Listening**. How well do I listen to understand what the person is really saying or concerned about? Do I listen attentively and not allow myself to be distracted? Do I really think other people are worth listening to? Do I ask questions to help me understand what the other person is saying? Is my body language and tone of voice open to and accepting of the other person or persons? Am I willing to invest time in this kind of listening?
_____	**2. Involving our employees in defining and solving a problem**. Do I come to discussions about defining and solving a problem with answers I want my employees to accept, or do I welcome honest and broad input which may change my initial ideas? Do I really think my employees have good ideas about how to get work done better, faster, and more effectively? Have I tapped into that knowledge base? Did it work? Am I willing to invest time in this type of group effort?
_____	**3. Not being afraid to be challenged by the people we manage**. Am I open and willing to change my mind based on the input of the people I manage? Am I afraid that I will look weak or indecisive if I change my mind? Do I sometimes feel pressured to make a decision immediately because someone else wants a decision now, even though I need more information or time to think about the information I already have?

4. Helping our people grow. What have I done to honestly assess the strengths and weaknesses of my employees? Have I talked with my employees about their growth and development desires? Have I assisted them in growing their talents and skills? Do I use discipline primarily as a teaching opportunity and not just to punish, embarrass, or make an example of an employee? Am I afraid that I will look weak if I do not publicly and angrily correct an employee?

5. Helping our people solve their work-related problems. Have I asked my employees in a non-threatening manner what they are struggling with in order to deal with a problem which hinders their own productivity and effectiveness, or of someone they manage? If so, have I made a deliberate effort on a timely basis to help them resolve the matter in a positive way?

6. Being friendly and genuinely respecting and caring for our employees. Do I genuinely respect my employees? Do I lose my temper from time to time? If so, do I raise my voice instead of remaining calm in dealing with the person and situation in a mature and calm manner? Am I friendly and kind to employees? And if so, am I also firm with them when necessary? Do I ask my employees about their outside of work interests? Do I take their individual and family health and other issues into account when necessary?

7. Treating everyone equitably and fairly. Am I perceived as favoring one or more employees over others? Do I show the same patience and understanding to everyone? Do I equitably share praise for work that is well done as an individual or a team? Do I give people who have messed up in the past a chance to improve themselves and make a contribution to the work team?

8. Always learning as broadly as possible. Do I have a plan to broaden my base of knowledge? What have I learned in the last week that was not work related and was new to me? Did I learn anything which was really fun and interesting? What was the source of my new learning (video, reading, conversation, meditation, etc.)? What would I really like to learn more about? Am I willing to invest time in broadening my base of learning?

9. Being a person of our word. Do I always do what I say I will do? Am I reliable and dependable? Do I get things done within the timeframe I promised? Do I tell the truth, even when it is unpleasant? Am I trustworthy?

10. Being healthy. Do I exercise regularly? If so, is it sufficient to keep me healthy or do I need to work towards a higher level of physical activity? If I do not exercise regularly, what is my plan to start a regular exercise program? Do I eat a healthy diet? If not, what is my plan to start a better diet? Do I do things which are relaxing and refreshing to my body and mind? Do I meditate regularly? If not, what is my plan to do so? Am I willing to invest time in getting healthier and staying healthier?

Weekly Plan

Now that you have rated yourself on these 10 Categories, pick out one or two things you want to start working on immediately. They can be the areas in which you scored lowest. They can be areas in which you are really excited to learn about and practice. Or they can be a mix of both.

Once you have picked the one or two areas in which you want to focus, write them down, and then underneath each item list one or two things you will do specifically to make progress in that area during the next week. For instance, for item #1, the Listening Category, you could write the following:

<u>Listening.</u>

1. <u>Eliminating Distractions:</u> Before talking with anyone in my office, I will make sure that I am totally focused on the person I am speaking with. I will not have any type of electronic media that I, or the person I am talking with, can be distracted by during our conversation. I will not answer a phone or text message. Ideally, I will turn off any electronic notification system that could interrupt our conversation. I will do this every day for a week.

2. <u>Understanding the Other Person:</u> When the other person starts to speak, I will not interrupt them until they are done speaking. If I do not understand everything they have said, I will ask them some questions so that I understand better what they are saying. If I think I understand what they are saying, I will state to them what I understand them to have said. I will do this every day for a week.

You should also devise some simple system which will regularly remind you throughout the week that these are the one or two items you are working on to improve your listening skills. The reminder system can be digitally based (see website and app information at the end of this chapter) or it can be as simple as a Post-it Note on your computer or smart phone screen. I have always found it helpful to have a yellow sticky note someplace where I will see it every day. My favorite sticky note, which I have used for years, is "Shut Up and Listen!" I have gotten to be a much better listener over the years, but I still need a not-too-subtle reminder to myself to make sure I am really listening to other individuals and/or groups.

What you choose to do the first week will probably need to be repeated for several weeks or even months in order to change your behavior in a positive way. As you review your behaviors each week, assess whether or not you need to continue working on that area or if you should work on one of the other 10 Categories.

Quarterly Review

In addition to developing our character, skills, and talents along the lines of the 10 Categories listed above, it is also important to take time on a quarterly basis to assess our progress as a manager and as an organization regarding the following goals:
- Bringing out the best in the people we manage
- Making better decisions
- Building employee commitment to each other and the organization
- Increasing productivity and effectiveness
- Increasing my job satisfaction.

Here is a tool you might find helpful to measure your progress in these important character-related management practices, organizational improvement, and job satisfaction.

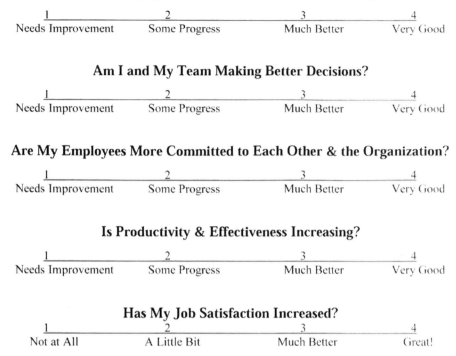

Am I Bringing Out the Best in the People I Manage?

1	2	3	4
Needs Improvement	Some Progress	Much Better	Very Good

Am I and My Team Making Better Decisions?

1	2	3	4
Needs Improvement	Some Progress	Much Better	Very Good

Are My Employees More Committed to Each Other & the Organization?

1	2	3	4
Needs Improvement	Some Progress	Much Better	Very Good

Is Productivity & Effectiveness Increasing?

1	2	3	4
Needs Improvement	Some Progress	Much Better	Very Good

Has My Job Satisfaction Increased?

1	2	3	4
Not at All	A Little Bit	Much Better	Great!

For additional assistance in assessing and improving your character, please go to the website for my book www.robertbeezat.com for an app to assist you.

CHAPTER TWELVE

SOME CONCLUDING THOUGHTS

Practice, Practice, Practice

Performing in Carnegie Hall in New York has been the goal of every great musician and vocal artist in the world for 125 years. A story goes that some tourists were looking for Carnegie Hall and met a man carrying a violin case. The couple did not know that he was one of the most talented and famous violinists in the world at the time. The tourist couple asked him, "How do you get to Carnegie Hall?" He quickly answered, "Practice, Practice, Practice!"

That same message is applicable to all of us as we work to improve our character, and it is something we all need to make a part of our lives no matter what we want to get better at.

Part of Aristotle's advice for growing in character centers on *practice and habit.* Just as someone who wants to play the piano, for example, must practice playing the piano, and the person who wants to be a better golfer, must practice golf, the person who wants to become a person of good character and good habits must practice good behaviors. As Aristotle puts it, "We become just by doing just actions, temperate by doing temperate actions, brave by doing brave actions." We can train our emotions and desires over time so that we take pleasure in doing just actions, just as we can train our bodies to take pleasure over time in certain types of physical exercise.

Create a Beautiful Organization

What do you think of when someone asks you what is beautiful?

I think of several things right off the bat: a beautiful woman, a beautiful sunset, a beautiful Puccini aria sung by Pavarotti, a beautiful scientific theory, a beautiful person, a beautiful landscape, a beautiful flower, a beautiful friendship… The list can go on and on.

So the question is, "What makes these things beautiful?"

My answer is that Beauty is the optimal harmony of the constituent parts of an entity.

Everything is made up of many elements. When those elements blend together at their highest level, we describe that entity as beautiful.

One very interesting thing about Beauty is that it isn't always tied to physical or material reality. We are able to perceive Beauty in many things that are not material in any way. For example, I always loved the idea that one of the tests of whether or not a scientist is on the right track in developing a theory is when the theory becomes beautiful. It is what the scientist usually means when she/he says that is everything comes together perfectly in the theory. It answers many questions in a cohesive and integrated way. And hence, the theory is beautiful!

Another example is to say that a friendship is beautiful. Again, there are many constituent elements that make up a beautiful friendship. Some of the elements are material and physical in nature, and some are the non-material personal relationships and bonds that exist between two friends.

I also find it interesting that Beauty is often associated with artistic work of various kinds. Why is Michelangelo's "David" a beautiful sculpture? Why is the ceiling of the Sistine Chapel considered a beautiful painting? Why is the Viet Nam Memorial Wall in Washington D.C. considered a beautiful work of architecture?

I think most people consider the above works of art to be beautiful because they capture both the physical/material elements of an entity as well as the spiritual/non-material. The elements are all combined into a wonderful harmony of the material and non-material. Certainly they are all portrayed in a material way, but they are beautiful because they capture the harmony, the convergence of both the material and the non-material aspects of reality.

Often artistic works of all types go beyond the mere representational. They create and reflect a reality which goes beyond the material. They creatively blend and harmonize many elements into a coherent and beautiful whole. We find them beautiful because they reach us at the deepest parts of who we are: material and spiritual beings.

A well-run organization is a thing of beauty. People who are part of the organization love to be part of it. Many aspects of their own work and the work of the organization as a whole just blend together so well. Those who do not work for the organization are drawn to it when opportunities arise for them to join the organization.

When I think of the beauty of an organization, I often think of Michael Jordan and how he led the Chicago Bulls to become one of the greatest teams ever. To see him play in a basketball game was to see an artist in action. "Air Jordan" is what we see when we think of him. It was artistry in motion and in the moment. It was artistry responding to an ever-changing environment each time he brought the basketball up the court. His personal and team statistics were impressive. But what captured people's imagination then, and still does now, is the image of "Air Jordan" creating many memorable works of athletic beauty and art.

Many people said Michael Jordan was so great because he was "gifted," which he was. But what people often did not know or think about when discussing how gifted Michael Jordan was, is the firm base he had in the fundamentals of his sport. He practiced as much or more than any other player.

And because he had such a firm grounding in the fundamentals of his sport, he could then improvise in awe-inspiring, jaw-dropping ways in response to whatever situation he faced on the basketball court.

His artistry helped every other member of his team excel to the highest level they could achieve. He brought out the best individual talents of his teammates, but even more importantly, his artistry was the key in creating an environment that resulted in one of the most successful teams in professional sports history.

Character And Spirituality (Some Considerations)

Developing and improving our character is not dependent on whether or not we believe that I and you in particular, and human beings in general, are a unique combination of matter and spirit. You can put into practice the ideas and suggestions in this book without thinking and believing that you are a material/spiritual being. If that is the case for you, you can skip this section and go to the last few pages of the book.

However, for me, spirituality is an element I consider in managing people. Here are some of my thoughts on the matter.

The great majority of world religious and philosophical systems are based on the idea that the universe is some type of combination of material and spiritual realities. A contrary and more recent view, particularly with the advent of science in the last few centuries, is that the universe is strictly a material reality.

I don't know which side of the argument is absolutely true. I don't think anyone really knows for sure. That matter is part of the reality is self-evident. Accidentally bang your knee on a desk corner and you will know that both you and the desk are material entities.

Less evident, but I think just as real, is that there is a spiritual component to reality. That understanding is based on my knowledge, experience, beliefs, and ability/capacity to love and be loved. I have written about this matter in greater detail in another book: *Knowing and Loving: The Keys to Real Happiness*. One of the chapters is titled "Why is There Something Instead of Nothing?" I don't have a definitive answer to that question. Again, no one does. But my answer is that there is some type of non-material/spiritual element which is part of each of us and the universe as a whole.

If, like me, you do think and believe that you, the people you manage and the universe as a whole have an element of spirit to it, here are some suggestions that I have found be helpful in developing my character. You may find them helpful also.

I Meditate and Pray

I meditate and pray because I know I am an imperfect being. I am good at a number of things, but I am not as good as I would like to be in many other things.

I think I have many good character traits which translate into good management, human relationship, communication, and decision-making practices and processes. But I know I sometimes fall short in these areas which, in turn, contribute to not bringing out the best in other people and do not make our working together as successful as possible.

I always want and welcome all the help I can get when doing anything.

Meditation and prayer are another source of help to me to be a person of better character and a better manager.

Meditation

Meditation helps me in many practical ways to deepen and synthesize my learning. It helps me see the connections between different aspects of reality, which in turn helps me and the people I manage to make better decisions.

In addition to these practical pluses of meditation, I think and believe that meditation helps me understand the inter-connectedness of all beings, and that we all progress or regress as people and organizations depending on how we see ourselves not only as individuals, which we are, but also as relational beings who grow and thrive together.

Allocating time for meditation on a regular basis (even 10 or 15 minutes a day) helps me grow my mind and my heart, which is so important in being a person of good character, and therefore, being a more successful manager.

Meditation is also quite relaxing and restorative to our minds and bodies. Life is busy, and trying to fit in 10 or 15 minutes of meditation seems difficult. But if you can make it a habit to meditate most days, you will find that it is a relaxing practice which fills you with energy and insight to accomplish the other things you need to do in your life.

Praying For Wisdom, Strength, and Courage

My first request is to ask for wisdom.

Wisdom is a combination of knowledge and love (head and heart) that leads to practical action.

I pray for knowledge as an aspect of wisdom to help me understand as much as I can about a situation, to correctly identify the problem and core issue, and to bring as broad an array of knowledge as I can and is relevant to the situation, taking into account a wide range of disciplines including, but not limited to: science, history, sociology, psychology, philosophy, economics, business, theology, etc.

I think that the more I know in as broad a range of relevant topics, the better decisions I can make.

I pray for and include love in my definition of wisdom because it adds a very important element to knowledge. I think that we know with both our head and our heart what love is. Love is part of wisdom, because it puts knowledge in perspective. Love speaks to the relational nature of people and things. Love is a choice, an act of will to choose the true, the good and the beautiful. Love helps me choose what is good for me and for others (they are usually not mutually exclusive goals).

Wisdom is the combination of mind and heart, which helps us choose what is right...what is good...what promotes life and love.

In addition to wisdom and finding a course of action which is best to pursue, I pray for strength and courage to actually do it.

Though strength and courage are similar in many ways, they mean two different things to me when I pray.

Strength is the capability to act:

- To start something.
- To see it through.
- To not give up prematurely just because it gets tough.

I pray for strength to go from a state of inertia to a course of action. Wisdom without strength doesn't get the job done.

Courage is related to strength because it often takes courage to do what wisdom leads us to do.

The wise decision may require a new course of action that others may consider foolish or a waste of time, or won't be successful. A wise course of action might actually cause people to want to harm us in some way. Sometimes it takes courage, because we may end up standing alone in our understanding of a situation and what we decide we should do about it. Sometimes it means risking failure.

So, I pray for courage.

I also pray for wisdom, strength and courage to protect me from my own stubbornness and bullheadedness, and sticking with a course of action until it hurts me or someone else. Wisdom knows when to stop a course of action if the circumstances change or we learn new things that should lead us to choose differently.

Our greatest strengths are also often our biggest weaknesses. Wisdom helps us see when our strength is killing us. It tells us when to change, what to change and how to change.

There are many prayers for wisdom, strength and courage in every faith tradition in the world. One of the best I have come across is an American Indian prayer called "The Great Spirit Prayer."

"Oh, Great Spirit, whose voice I hear in the wind,

Whose breath gives life to all the world.

Hear me;

I need your strength and wisdom.

Let me walk in beauty, and make my eyes ever behold the red and purple sunset.

Make my hands respect the things you have made and my ears sharp to hear your voice

Make me wise so that I may understand the things you have taught my people.

Help me to remain calm and strong in the face of all that comes towards me.

Let me learn the lessons you have hidden in every leaf and rock.

Help me seek pure thoughts and act with the intention of helping others.

Help me find compassion without empathy overwhelming me.

I seek strength, not to be greater than my sister or brother, but to fight my greatest enemy

Myself.

Make me always ready to come to you with clean hands and straight eyes.

So when life fades, as the fading sunset, my spirit may come to you without shame.

There are also two shorter prayers which I say many times on some days, particularly when I will be involved in meetings with a number of people so that all of us will bring our best selves to the meeting and that our work together will be productive.

The first is a prayer to be led along a path which will use the best of our hearts and minds, and will lead us to joy in positive accomplishments.

God, Who by the light of the Holy Spirit

did instruct the hearts of Your faithful people,

grant us by that same Spirit to be truly wise in all things,

and to rejoice in the good You lead us to do.

The second prayer is even shorter:

Come Holy Spirit, fill the hearts of Your faithful people, and

Kindle in us the fire of love.

Send us Your Spirit

And together, we shall renew the face of the earth.

Managing a successful organization requires that managers be well-grounded in their job process skills and job knowledge. But the beauty and artistry of the manager comes from how they creatively integrate their interpersonal behaviors with their process skills and job knowledge to create a beautiful and successful outcome on an on-going basis in response to the ever-changing environment in which we do our work. That idea of creating beauty and success as an organization brings us back to the following chart:

CHARACTER BASED MANAGEMENT

A Good & Successful Manager Must Integrate

Inter-Personal Behaviors	Process Skills	Job Knowledge
Values	Planning	Product or Service
Habits/Virtues	Communicating	Personnel
Character	Leading	Finance
Growth	Team Building	Technology
Continuous Learning	Organizing/	Marketing & Sales
Dealing With	Re-Organizing	Legal
Uncertainty	Managing Risk	

Integrating all of these elements and factors is a challenge, but managers of good character do this well and do it often. They help create a thing of beauty that maximizes the contributions of all the people they manage, and which meets the needs of their customers or clients.

Have Fun!Celebrate!

Getting better at anything in life takes work. But it is good to remind ourselves that hard work does not preclude having fun. Humor is very hard to define, but we know it when we see or experience it. Injecting some humor in our everyday efforts to improve ourselves and our organization can increase everyone's job satisfaction. But humor should not be forced. It should flow from our interpersonal relationships with the people we manage and the situations that we deal with together. There are plenty of occasions when the ironies of life, from both a personal and organizational standpoint, can be very humorous.

Being able to laugh at ourselves is important to our own well-being. Some self-deprecating humor can ease friction between people in an organization. It makes the manager human. It helps put employees at ease, which in turn will encourage them to be relaxed and open to sharing their ideas with you as the manager and with their fellow employees.

On the other hand, a manager should never, ever, make fun of an employee or a joke at her or his expense.

Take time to celebrate individual and group accomplishments. Most people enjoy that. Employees usually will not do that unless their manager sets the proper tone. Once it becomes a habit to celebrate individual and group accomplishments, employees will keep the ball rolling.

Be Of Good Cheer! Enjoy Your Work!

Being a manager is a wonderful way to use all of your talents, skills and abilities as set forth in this book. There is a great deal of professional and personal satisfaction in doing a job well.

I hope you develop a Dream Team of your own.

As you grow your good character, you will also find that the work you and the people you manage do every day succeeds to a higher degree than it has in the past.

You will be a better person, not only at work, but in the rest of your life as well.

CPSIA information can be obtained at www.ICGtesting.com
Printed in the USA
LVOW11s0054220716

497334LV00001B/96/P